Reception English is a breeze with CGP!

This book has been carefully written to provide stacks of questions for Reception pupils. It covers all the important topics, including Phonics and Writing. It's never been easier to help pupils become confident in English.

But wait, there's more! You'll find handy progress tests at the end of each section to check how pupils are getting on. Plus, we've included answers at the back of the book to make things extra easy.

What CGP is all about

Our sole aim here at CGP is to produce the highest quality books — carefully written, immaculately presented and dangerously close to being funny.

Then we work our socks off to get them out to you — at the cheapest possible prices.

Contents

Section One — Reading

Published by CGP

Editors:
Aimee Ashurst, Keith Blackhall, Andy Cashmore, Emma Crighton and Emma Duffee.

ISBN: 978 1 83774 051 2

With thanks to Catherine Heygate and Lucy Towle for the proofreading.
With thanks to Jade Sim for the copyright research.

Images on the cover and throughout the book © Educlips
Clipart from Corel®

Printed by Zenith Print & Packaging Ltd, Pontypridd.
Based on the classic CGP style created by Richard Parsons.

CGP, Broughton House, Griffin Street, Broughton-in-Furness, Cumbria, LA20 6HH.
EU Rep: International Associates Auditing & Certification Limited, The Black Church, St Mary's Place,
Dublin 7, D07 P4AX, Ireland. EUAR@ie.ia-net.com

About This Book

This Book is Full of Reception English Questions

This book has questions for the topics in Reception English.
It covers reading (including phonics) and writing.

Some pages have
Warm Up Questions
to get you started
on the topic.

There are Three Tests in This Book

There are some Before You Start questions to complete at the front
of the book so you can see what you already know about English.

There are two Progress Tests. Each one
tests you on the topics that have come
before it. They help you see how you're
doing with the topics covered so far.

Colour the Smiley Face at the End of Each Topic

There is a smiley face at the end of each topic.

Colour the smiley face to show that you've completed
the questions on those pages bond are ready to move on.

Great job! Colour the smiley face. 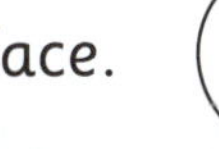

Before You Start

(1) **Say** what you **see**.
Colour all the animals.

3 marks

(2) **Look** at the picture in the box. Circle one thing that starts with the **same sound**.

1 mark

(3) **Tick** the picture that starts with the **m** sound.

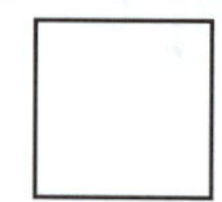

1 mark

Before You Start

4 **Circle** the picture that starts with the **p** sound.

1 mark

5 **Look** at the picture below.
Circle the thing that does **not** belong.

1 mark

6 Carefully **draw lines** to join the red dots.

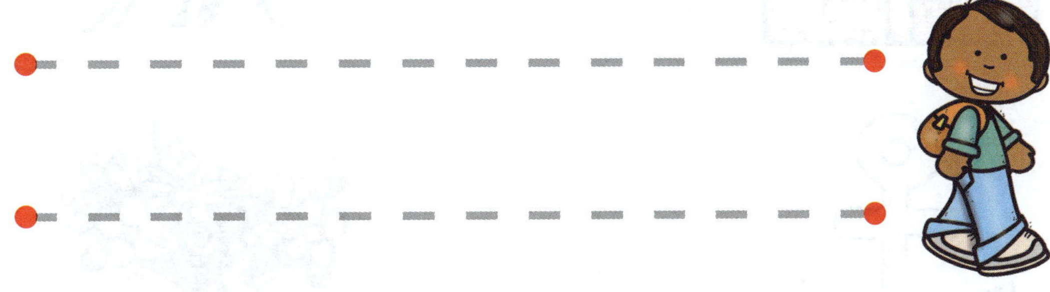

2 marks

Score: ___ /9

s, a and t

1   **Circle** the picture that **starts** with the **s** sound.

2   **Colour in** the picture that **starts** with the **t** sound.

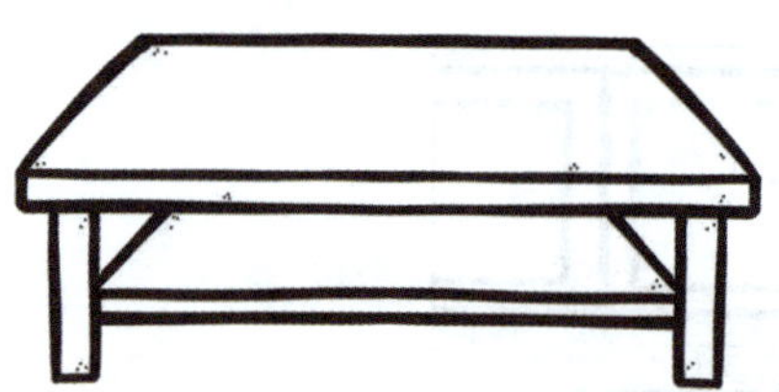  

3   Put a **tick** next to the pictures that **start** with the **a** sound.

    Great job! Colour the smiley face.

p, i and n

1 Put a **tick** under the picture that **starts** with the **p** sound.

2 **Look** at the picture.
Circle the letter that the word **begins** with.

3 Say the sound that each word **starts** with.
Then **write** the **letter** for that sound.
Choose from these letters: **p**, **n** and **i**.

Great job! Colour the smiley face. 

m, d and g

Warm Up Question

Which picture **starts** with the **m** sound?
Draw a line to match it to the **m**.

m

1   Put a **tick** next to the picture that **starts** with the **d** sound.

2   **Say** the sound the letter makes. **Circle** the picture that **starts** with that letter.

m

g

d

m

Great job! Colour the smiley face.

o, c and k

(1) **Draw** lines to match each picture to the letter it **starts** with.

o

c

(2) **Colour** the picture that **starts** with the **k** sound.

(3) Look at each picture. Say the sound the word **starts** with. **Circle** the letter that **starts** the word.

c   o

k   o

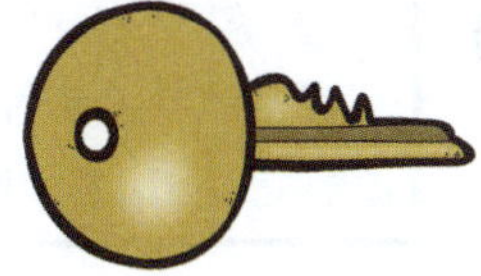

o   k

c   o

Great job! Colour the smiley face.

ck, e and u

1 Say what you see. **Circle** all the things that **end** with **ck**.

2 Look at each picture. **Write** the **missing** letter. Choose from these letters: **e** and **u**.

 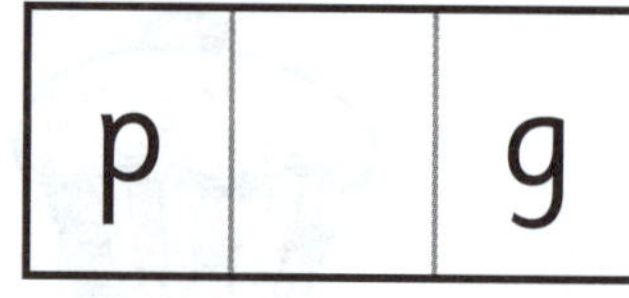  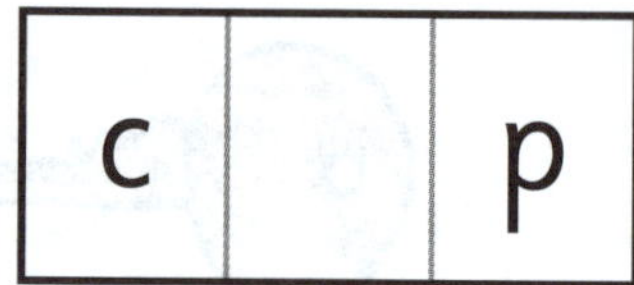

Great job! Colour the smiley face.

r, h and b

Which **colour starts** with the **r** sound?
Draw a line to match it to the **r**.

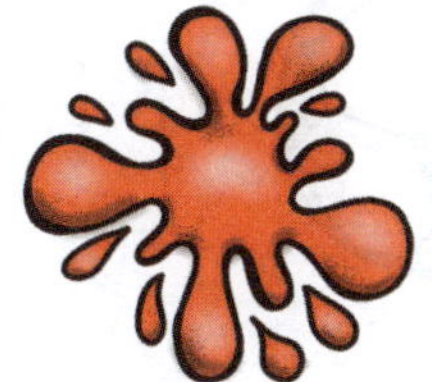  

1   **Tick** the pictures that **start** with the **h** sound.

 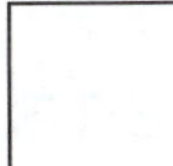 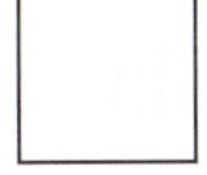

2   **Say** the sound that each word **starts** with.
Then **write** the **letter** for that sound.
Choose from these letters: **r**, **h** and **b**.

Great job! Colour the smiley face.

f, l, ff, ll and ss

(1) Look at each picture. **Say** the sound the word **starts** with. **Circle** the letter that **starts** the word.

(2) **Colour** the picture that **ends** with **ll**.

(3) **Draw** lines to match each picture to the letters it **ends** with.

Great job! Colour the smiley face. 

j, v and w

Put a **tick** next to the picture that **starts** with the **v** sound.

  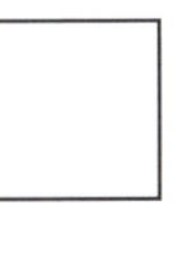  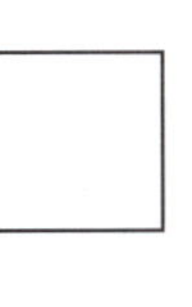

1 Say the sound the letter makes. **Circle** the picture that **starts** with that letter.

v  

w  

w  

j  

2 Say the sound that each word **starts** with. Then **write** the letter for that sound. Choose from these letters: **j**, **v** and **w**.

Great job! Colour the smiley face.

x, y, z and zz

(1) **Circle** the picture that **ends** with the **x** sound.

(2) **Draw** lines to match each picture to the letter it **starts** with.

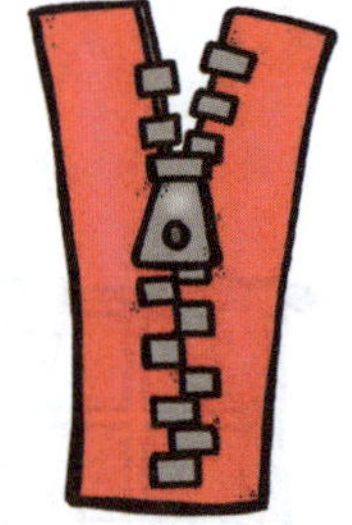

y

z

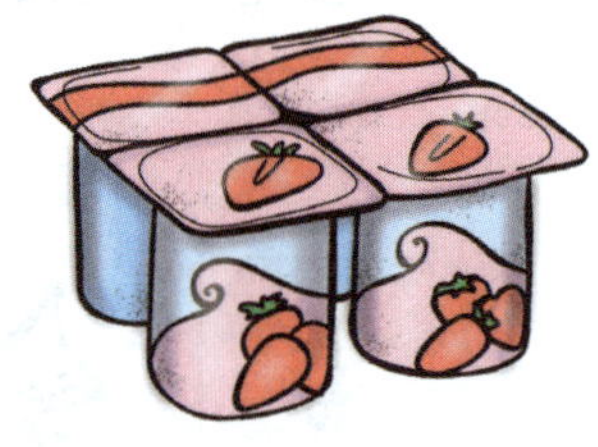

(3) Look at the pictures. **Write** the missing letters to **complete** each word.

x   y   zz

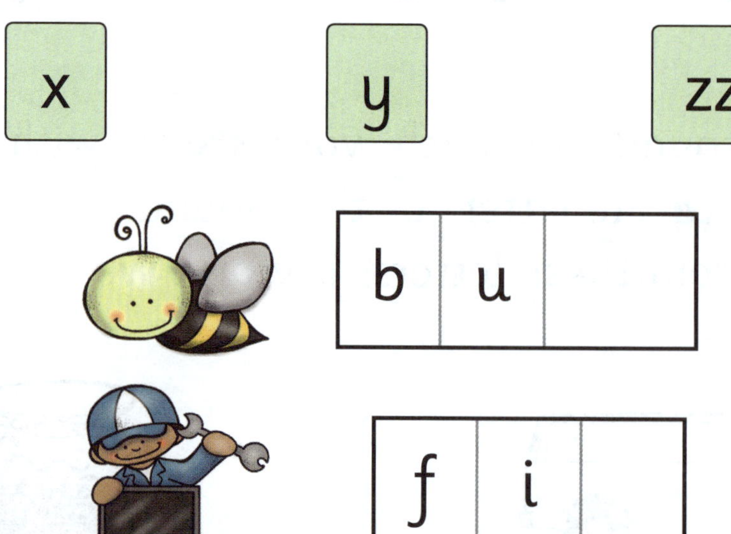

| b | u | |

| f | i | |

Great job! Colour the smiley face.

qu, ch and sh

Warm Up Question

Circle the picture that **starts** with **qu**.

1 Say what you see. **Colour** the two **letters** that make the sound at the **start** of the word.

 ch | sh

ch | sh

 ch | sh

 ch | sh

2 **Sound out** each word. **Colour** the correct word for the picture.

quack  quick

Great job! Colour the smiley face.

th, ng and nk

① **Colour** the picture that **ends** with **th**.

② **Tick** the picture that **ends** with **ng**.

 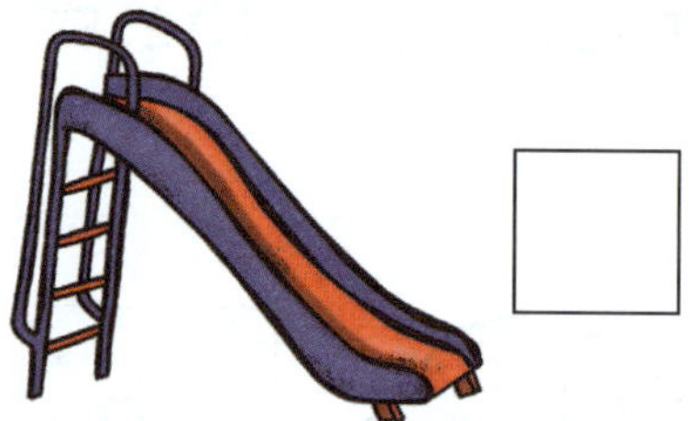

③ Say the sound that these two letters make: **nk**.
Circle the **two** pictures that **end** with this sound.

 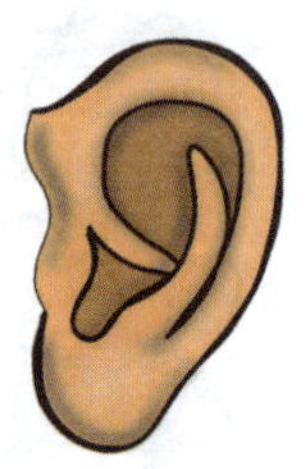 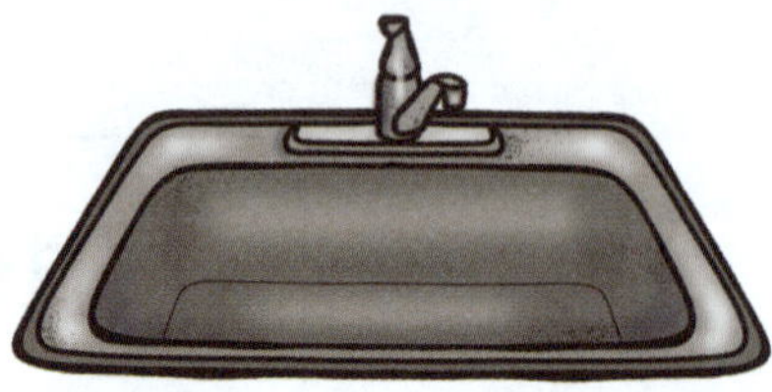

Great job! Colour the smiley face.

Word Practice

1 Sound out the words. **Draw** lines to match each word to the right picture.

log   map   pin

2 Choose the letter that completes the word. **Write** the letter in the word frame.

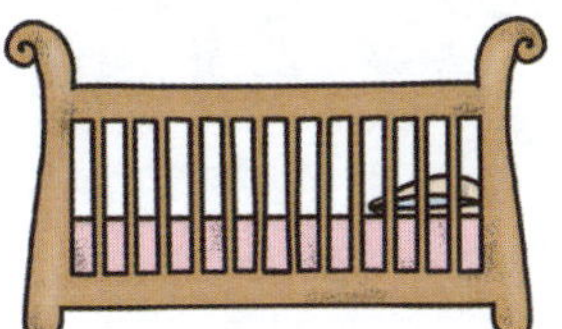

| c | o | |

b   t

| b | a | |

ck   g

| d | o | |

ll   th

Word Practice

3 Read the caption. **Circle** the best picture for the caption.

hot mug

a red pen

a dog in a box

4 **Tick** the caption that matches each picture.

Ella is ill ☐

Ella kicks it ☐

dig in the mud ☐

hop on the bus ☐

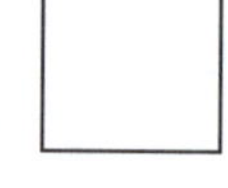

Word Practice

5 Read each caption. **Draw** lines to match it to the correct picture.

big bug

six cans

on a log

6 Look at the picture. Use the **letters** to **make** the word.

w b e

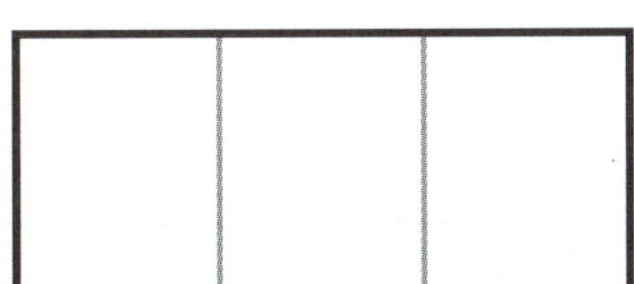

ch n i

o sh p

Great job! Colour the smiley face.

Tricky Words

1 Read each caption. **Colour** the picture that **matches** the caption.

his cat

top of the hill

2 Read each caption. **Draw** lines to match each one to the correct picture.

I sing

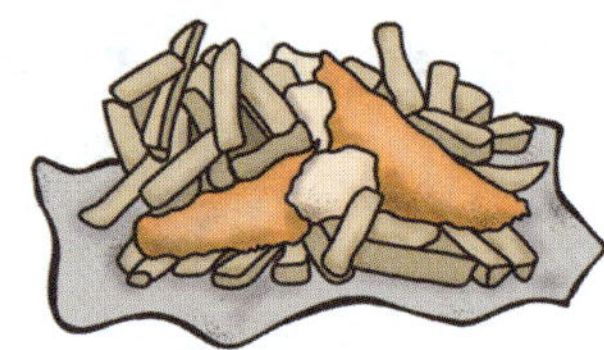

her ship

fish and chips

no hats

Tricky Words

3 Read each sentence. **Circle** the best picture for the sentence.

She is sad.

Go into the hut.

4 **Copy** one of the tricky words below to complete each caption.

as   to   we

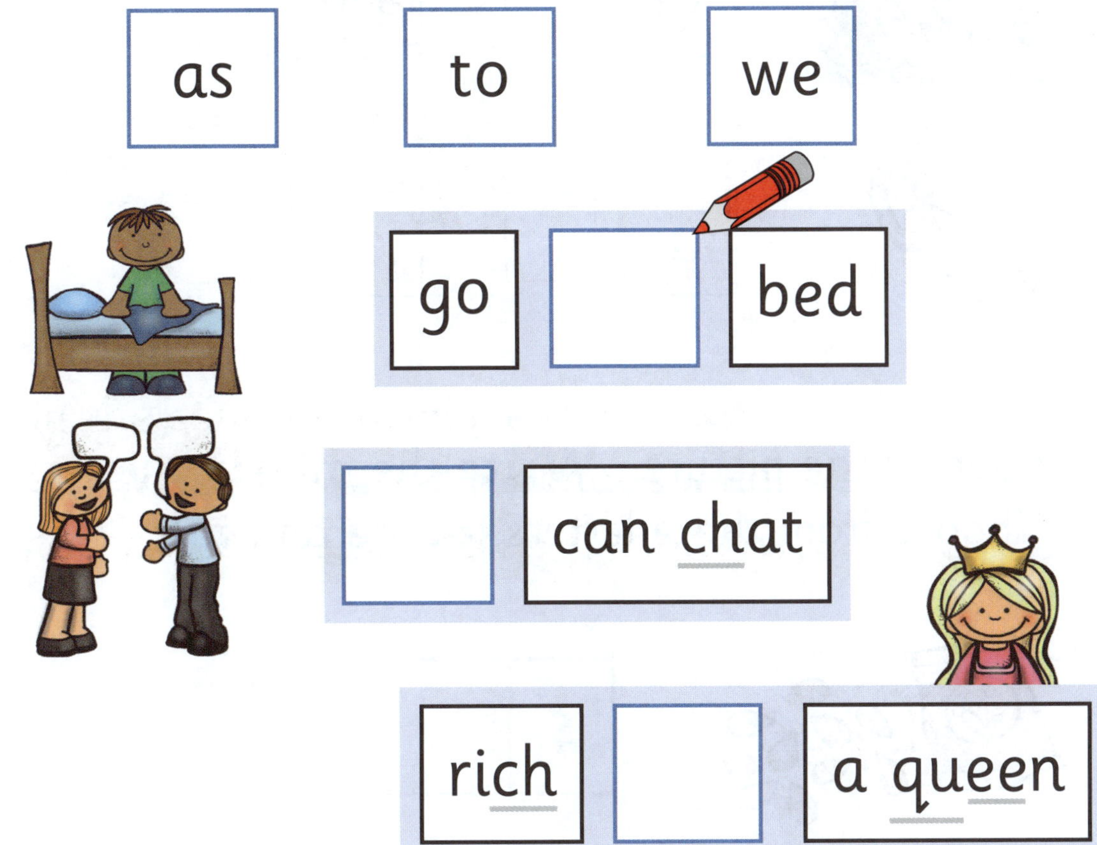

Great job! Colour the smiley face. 

ai, ee and igh

Warm Up Question

Circle the picture that has **ai** in it.

1 **Say** the word for the picture.
What sound can you hear in the **middle** of the word? Put a **tick** next to the letters.

 ai ☐ igh ☐

 ai ☐ ee ☐

2 Look at the picture. **Write** the **missing** letters.
Choose from these letters: **ai**, **ee** and **igh**.

s		d

Great job! Colour the smiley face.

oa, oo and ar

(1) Sound out each word.
Colour the picture that **matches** the word.

goat   

moon 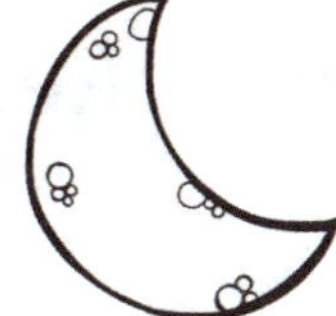 

foot 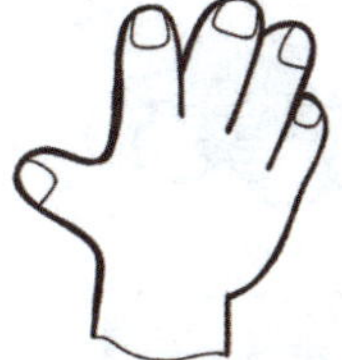 

(2) Look at the picture. Then use the letters to **make** a word.

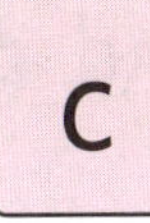 d   c   ar  

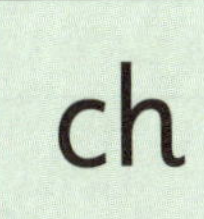 ar   ch   m  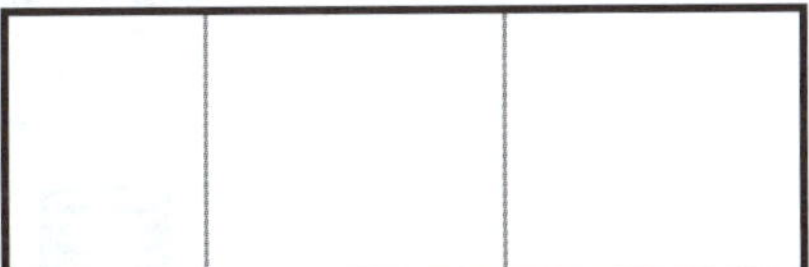

Great job! Colour the smiley face. ☺

or, ur, ow and oi

1 Which picture has **or** in it?
Draw a line to match it to the letters.

 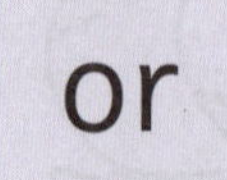 

2 **Circle** the word that **matches** the picture.

burn  born

oil  owl

3 Look at the pictures, then **write** the **missing** letters.
Choose from these letters: **or**, **ur**, **ow** and **oi**.

s		l

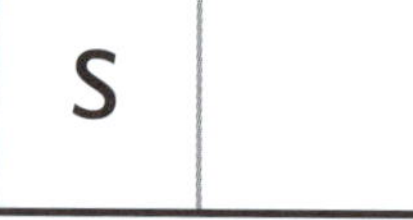

c		n	s

          Great job! Colour the smiley face.

ear, air and er

1 **Circle** the picture that has the 'ear' sound.

 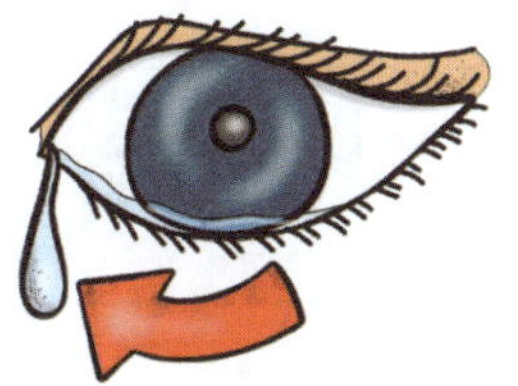 

2 Sound out the words. **Draw** lines to match each word to the right picture.

| hair | pair | fair |

3 Look at the picture. Use the **letters** to **make** the word. Then **write** the word in the word frame.

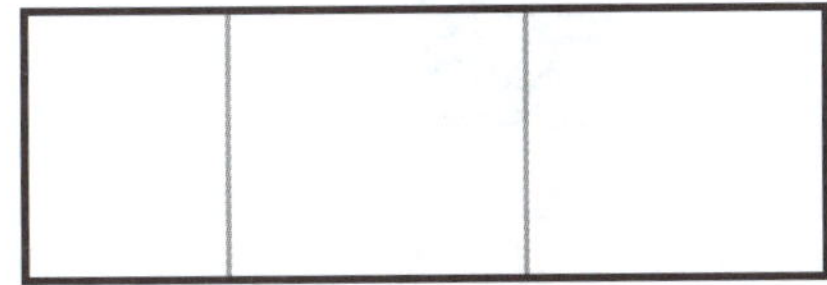

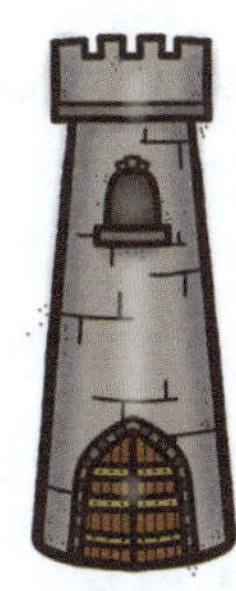

Great job! Colour the smiley face.   😊

Words and Sentences

Warm Up Question

Colour the caption that **matches** the picture.

her burger

visit the zoo

1   **Draw** lines to **match** each caption to the best picture.

his dark lair

a pair of peppers

2   **Circle** the picture that **matches** each sentence.

I am in the rain.

Meg misses her coat.

The lord is in the fort.

Words and Sentences

3 **Write** each sentence in the word frames.

She has boxes.

She

Look at a farm.

4 Say what you see. Then **write** the letters in the word frames. Use each letter **once**.

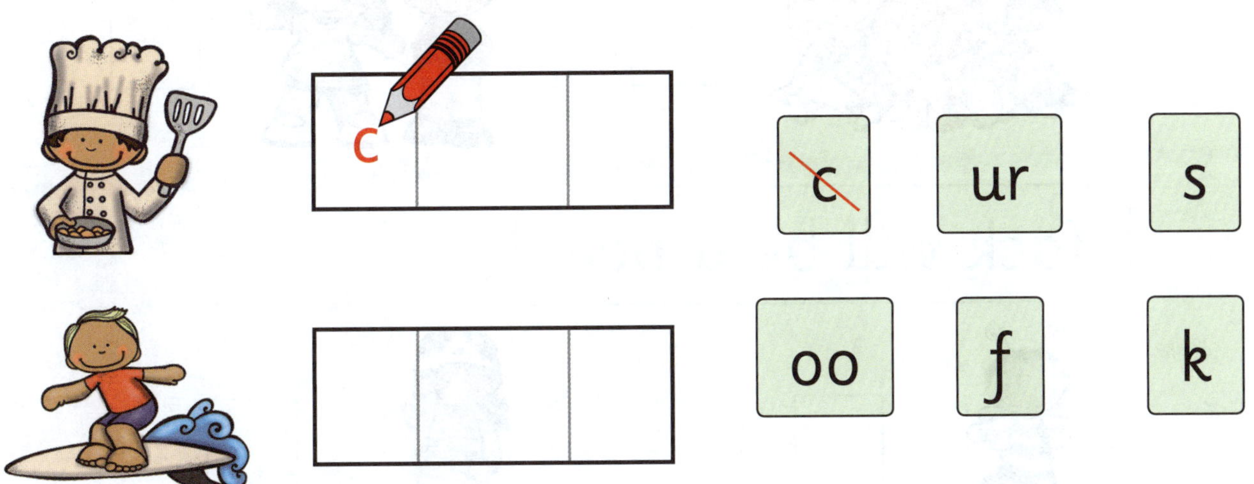

Great job! Colour the smiley face.

More Tricky Words

1   **Circle** the picture that matches each word.

me

sure

pure

2   **Tick** the picture that matches the sentence.

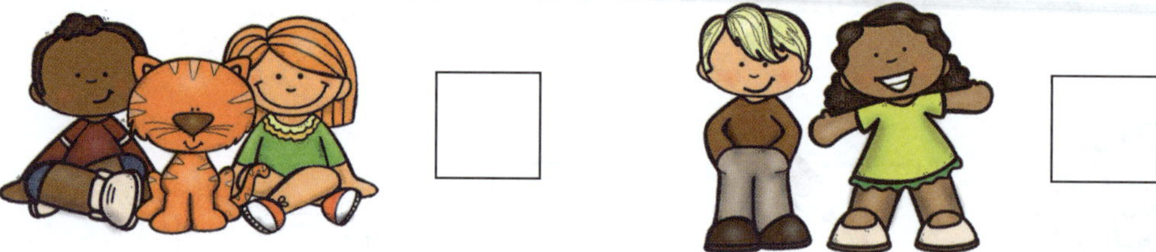

All of us sit down.

Jack will be a bee.

More Tricky Words

3 **Read** each sentence. **Draw** a line to match it to the best picture.

They can go high.

They are at the shop.

4 **Copy** one of the tricky words below to complete each sentence.

| my | you | was |

I sit on [ ] chair.

Can [ ] see it?

The car [ ] pink.

Great job! Colour the smiley face. 

Words with Extra Consonants

Circle the picture that **matches** the word.

trunk

(1) **Draw** a line to match each word to the best picture.

clap   melt   hump   stair

 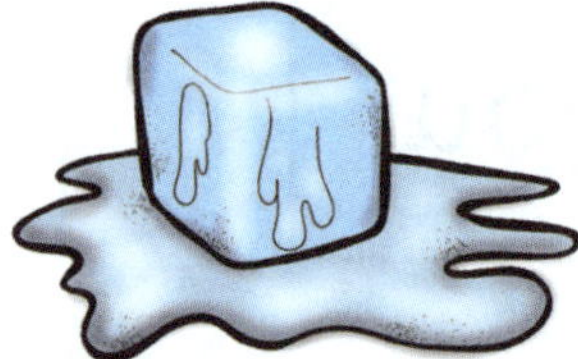 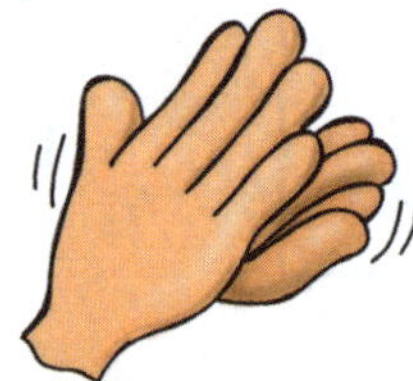 

(2) **Colour** the word that **matches** each picture.

street      strap

crust   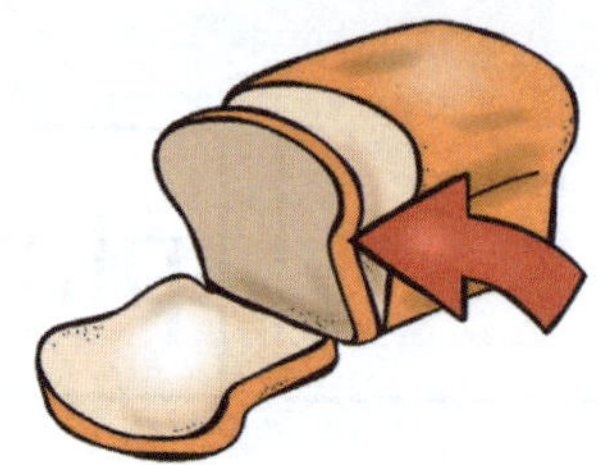   trust

Section One — Reading

Words with Extra Consonants

3   **Tick** the word that **matches** each picture.

4   **Look** at the pictures. **Read** the captions.
Circle the best caption for the pictures.

5   Look at each picture.
Use the letters to make each word.

Great job! Colour the smiley face.

More Words and Sentences

1 Sound out the words. **Draw** lines to match each word to the right picture.

jumping   painted   longest

2 Say the word. Then **add** a letter to the **start** to make a word that matches the picture. Choose from these letters: **s**, **g** and **t**.

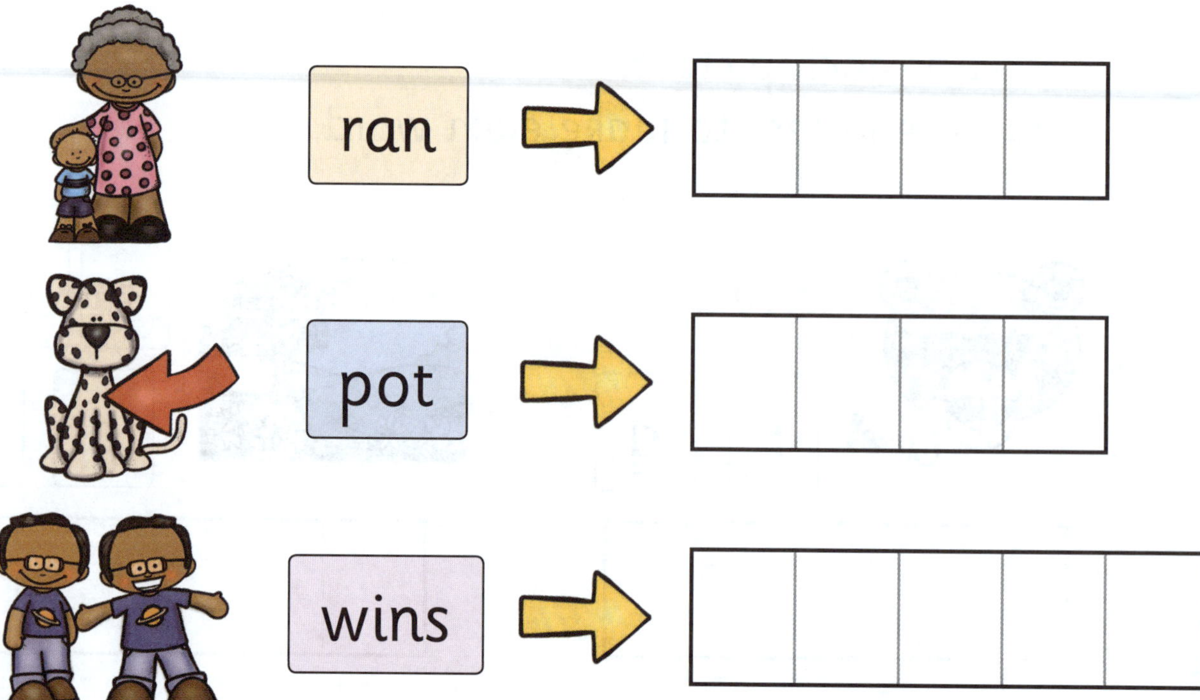

More Words and Sentences

(3) Read each sentence. **Circle** the best picture for the sentence.

I spot stars.

We can turn.

It's so little.

(4) **Add** the ending. Then **write** the **new** word.

 sink ➕ ing 

 sleep ➕ ing 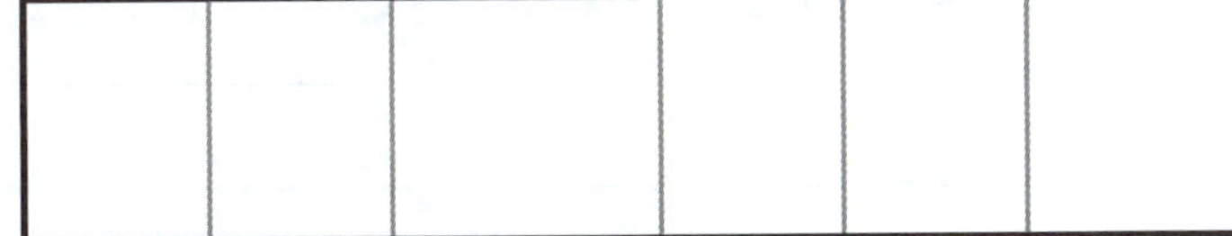

Great job! Colour the smiley face. ☺

More Tricky Words

Colour in the caption that **matches** the picture.

| some sweets |  | some crisps |

---

(1) **Tick** the best picture for each caption.

one starfish  ☐ 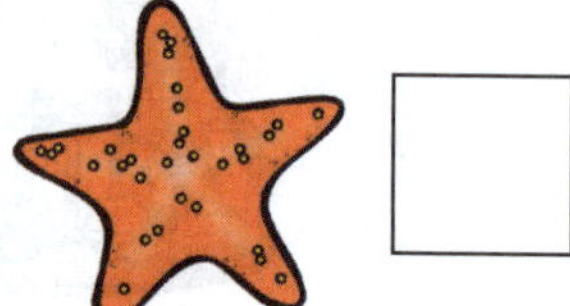 ☐

a little splat 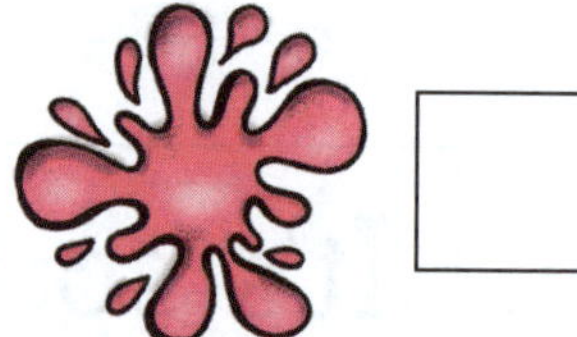 ☐ 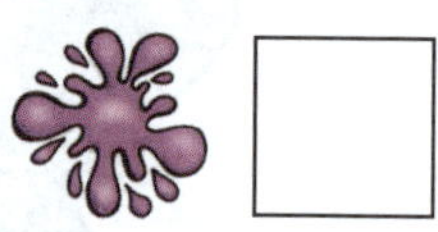 ☐

(2) **Write** each sentence in the word frames.

I have a rabbit. 

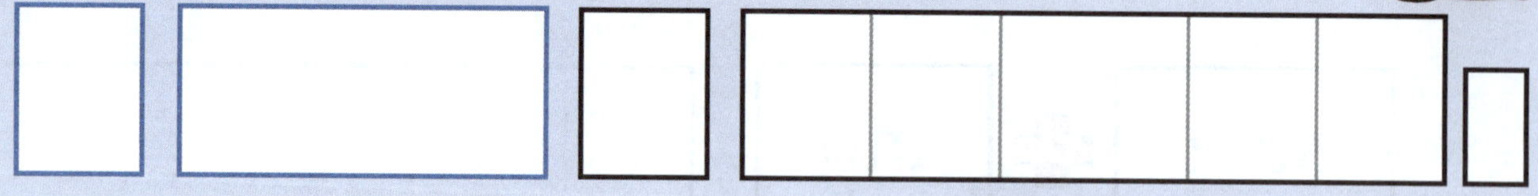

What do you see? 

More Tricky Words

3 **Circle** the picture that **matches** each caption.

| he says yes |

| there is my quilt |

| when it is hot |

4 **Copy** one of the words to complete each sentence.

| said | love | were |

She ________ so. 

They ________ sad. 

I ________ my dress. 

Great job! Colour the smiley face. 🙂

Understanding Stories

Read the speech bubbles. **Circle** the alien named **Blurf**.

Have a look at this story.

 **Where** did the aliens land? **Circle** your answer.

Understanding Stories

2 How did the aliens **feel** about the planet when they landed? Circle **one** face.

3 Why did the aliens leave? **Colour** one sentence.

They had a fright.	It was boring.

Here is another alien planet.

4 Do you think the green aliens from the story would like this planet? **Circle yes** or **no**.

Yes   No

Understanding Stories

Read the sentences about the band.

This is my jazz band. Yaz sings. I have the trumpet. Asha is the drummer.

(5) Who do you think is **Asha**? **Tick** your answer.

(6) **Colour in** the instrument that is **not** in the band.

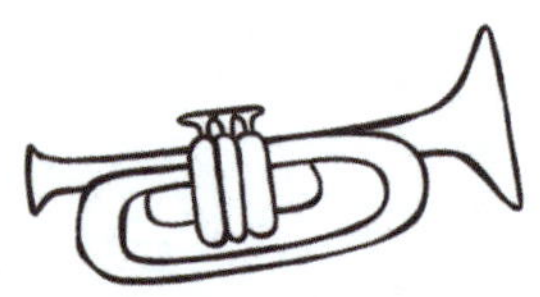  

Understanding Stories

Read the story below.

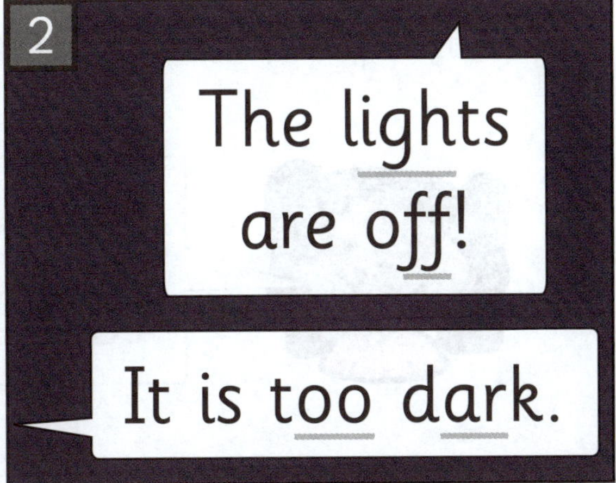

(7) Do you think the audience likes the band?
Circle yes or **no**.

Yes   No

(8) **Circle** the object that saves the show.

  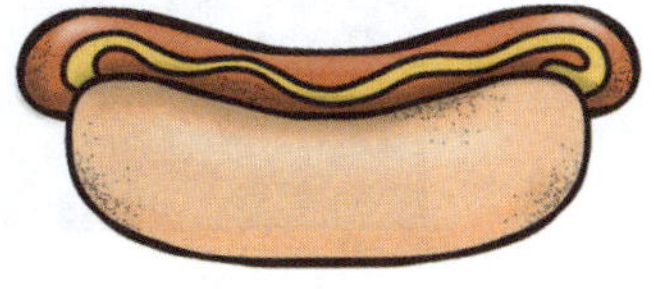

Great job! Colour the smiley face. 

What Happens Next?

(1) **Read** the speech bubble. What do you think will happen **next**? **Tick** the right picture.

(2) **Look** at the picture and **read** what Alex and his dad say. **Colour** in the place you think they will go **next**.

What Happens Next?

3   **Read** the speech bubble. What do you think will happen **next**? **Draw** a line to match the girl to the right picture.

4   **Read** Ali's packing list. Can you work out where he is going? **Circle** your answer.

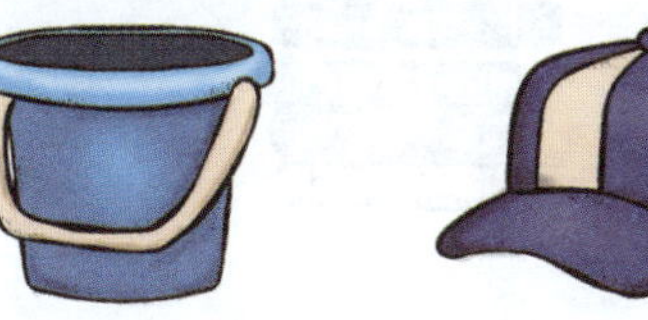

Great job! Colour the smiley face. 

Progress Test 1

Read the sentences in the bubbles and look at the picture.

1 What time of year do you think it is in the picture? Put a **tick** next to your answer.

 winter ☐    summer ☐

1 mark

2 Here are some objects from the park. **Draw** lines to match each word to the correct picture.

books

tree

1 mark

Progress Test 1

3 Who do you think might want to have a rest? **Circle** your answer.

1 mark

4 **Colour** the pictures that contain the **ee** sound.

2 marks

5 **Tick** the caption that matches the picture.

He loves the swing. ☐

He is running. ☐

1 mark

6 **Colour** the word that is missing from the sentence.

I will go ___ the park.

to   do

1 mark

Score: ☐/7

Lines and Loops

Warm Up Question

Trace the lines to join the red dots.

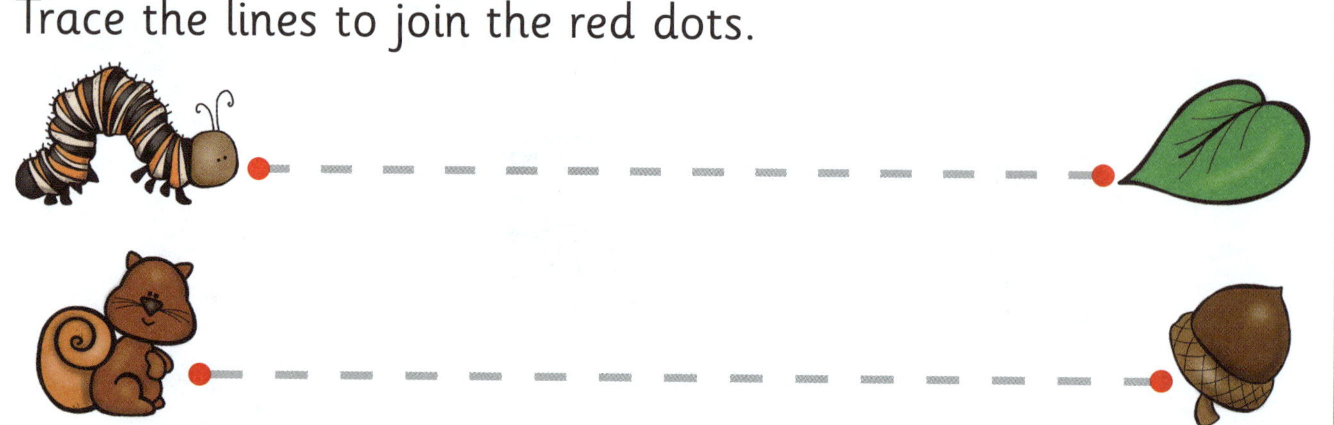

1. **Trace** the lines to join the animal to its home.

2. **Trace** the loops to join the **green** dots.

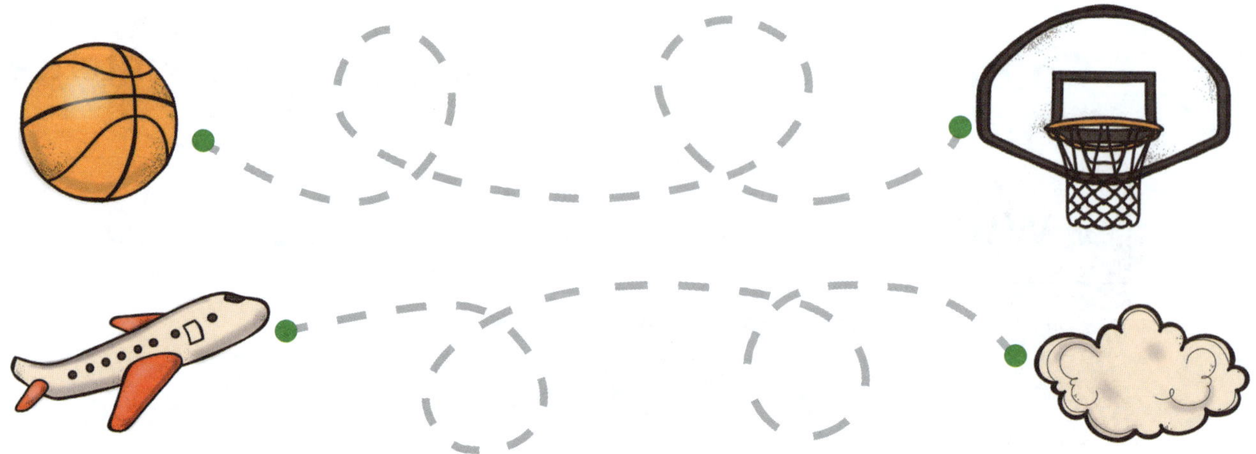

Lines and Loops

(3) **Trace** the line to show the boat's journey.

(4) **Trace** the lines to finish the picture.

Great job! Colour the smiley face.

c, o and a

1 **Start** at the **red** dots and **trace** the letters. Practise writing the letters **c**, **o** and **a**.

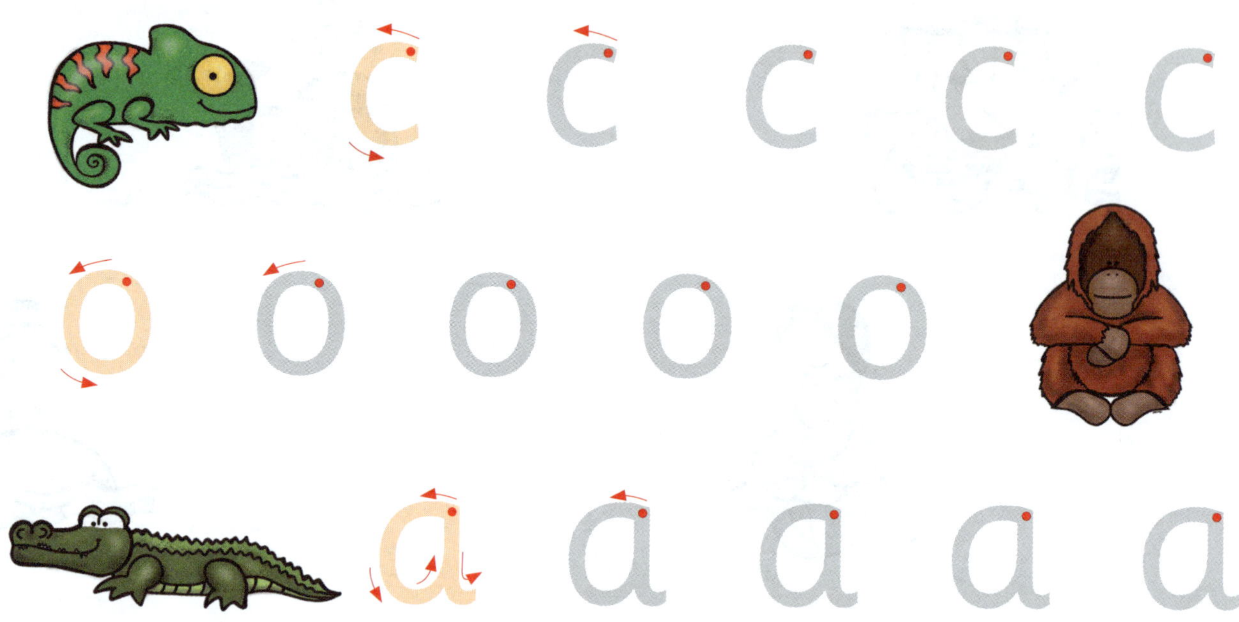

2 **Trace** the letters as neatly as you can.

Great job! Colour the smiley face. 

i, l and t

1 Practise writing the letters **i**, **l** and **t**.

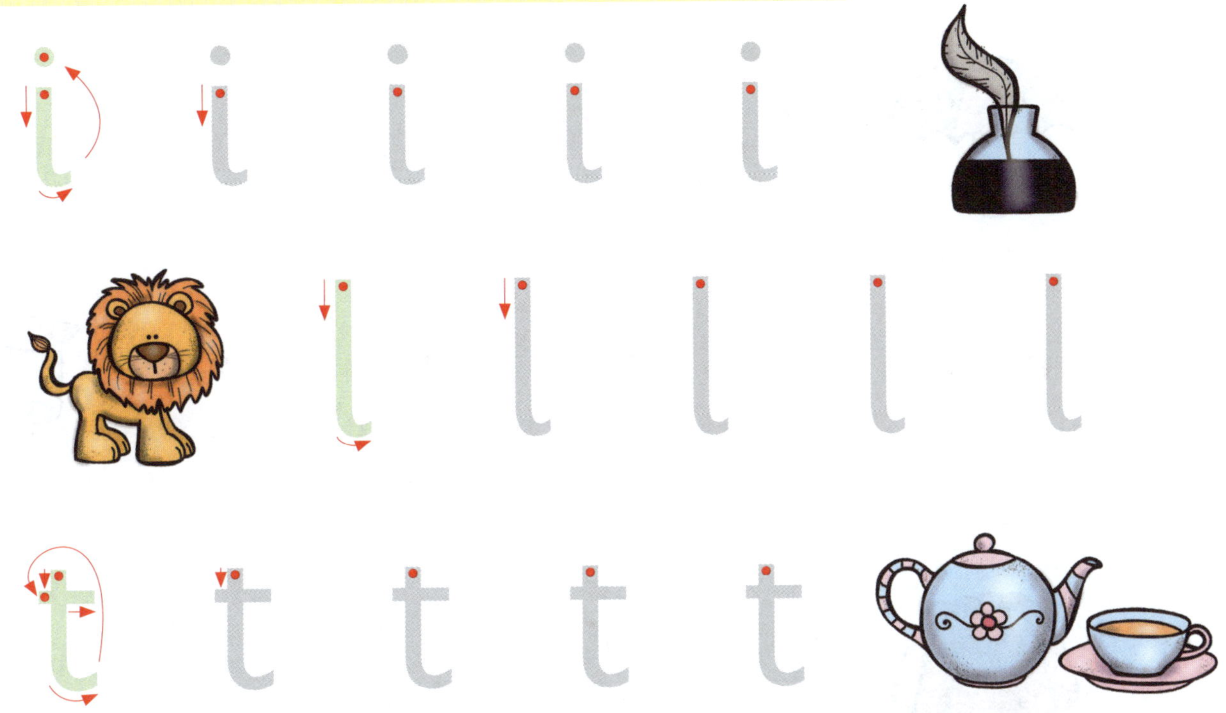

2 Trace the missing letters to **finish** these words.

Great job! Colour the smiley face. 

u, y and j

1 Start at the red dots to write **u**, **y** and **j**.

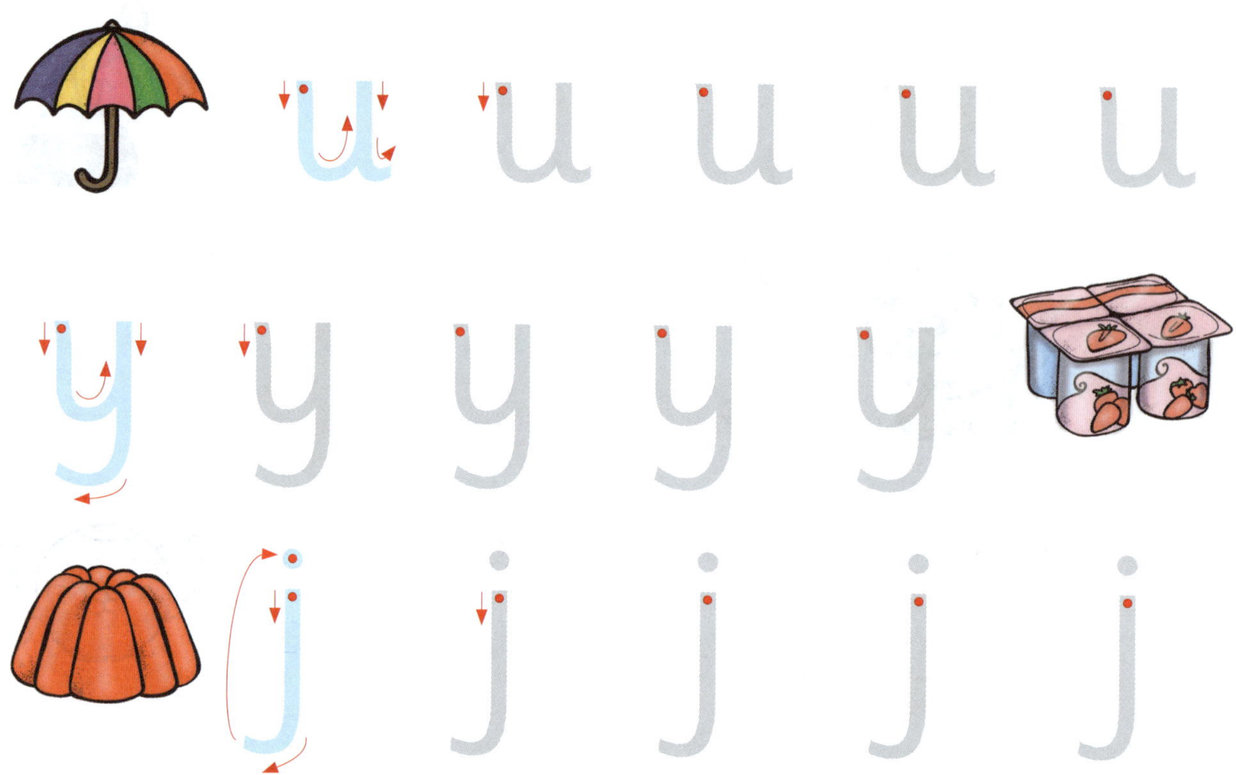

2 These words have some letters missing.
Trace the letters to **finish** the words.

Section Two — Writing

Great job! Colour the smiley face.

r, n and m

1 Follow the arrows to write **r**, **n** and **m**.

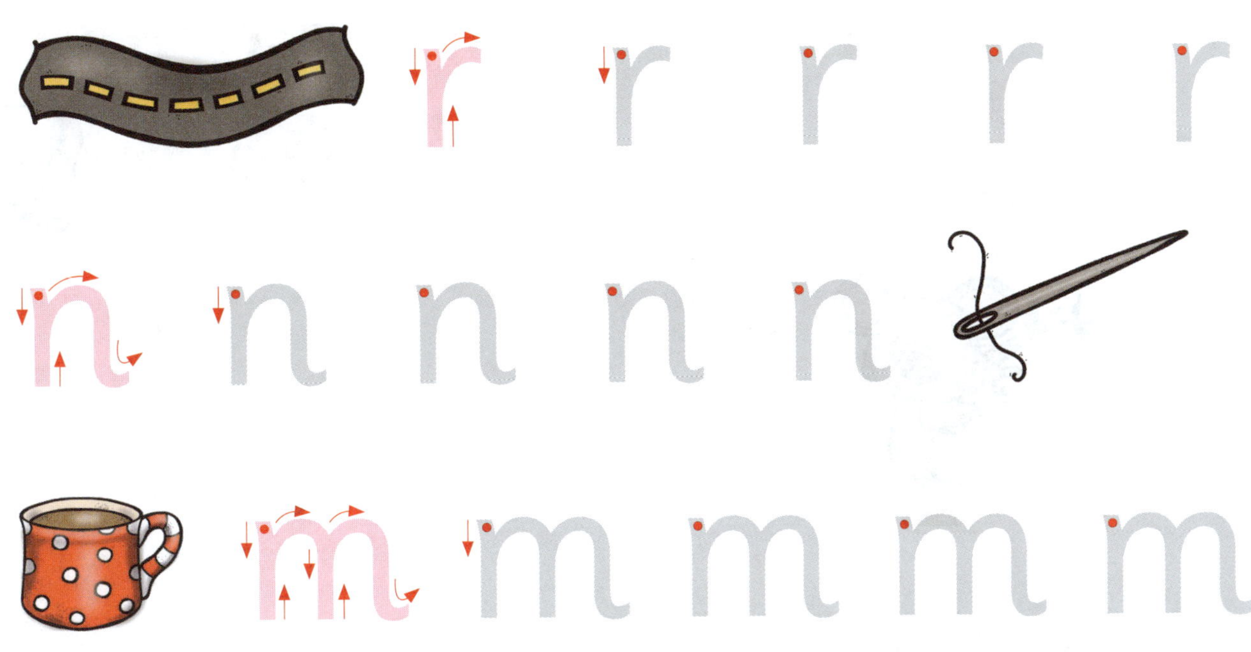

2 **Complete** the words by **tracing** the missing letters as neatly as you can.

Great job! Colour the smiley face. 

h and k

(1) Practise writing the letters **h** and **k**.

(2) **Fill in** the missing letters. **Draw** lines to match each word to the right picture.

hush

kick

chick

Great job! Colour the smiley face.

b and p

1 Practise writing the letters below.

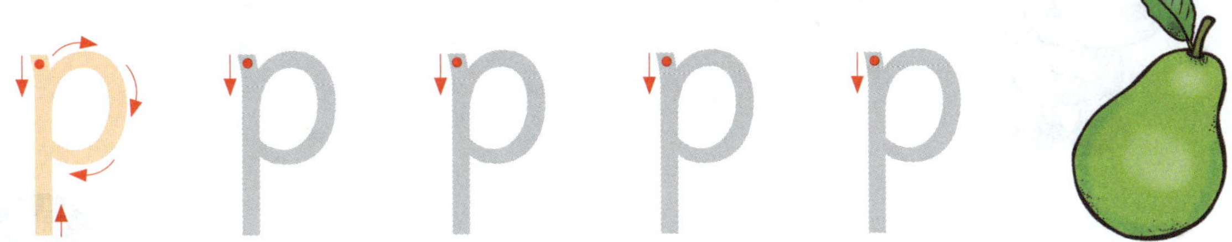

2 Fill in the missing letters.
Then **colour in** the pictures.

ball

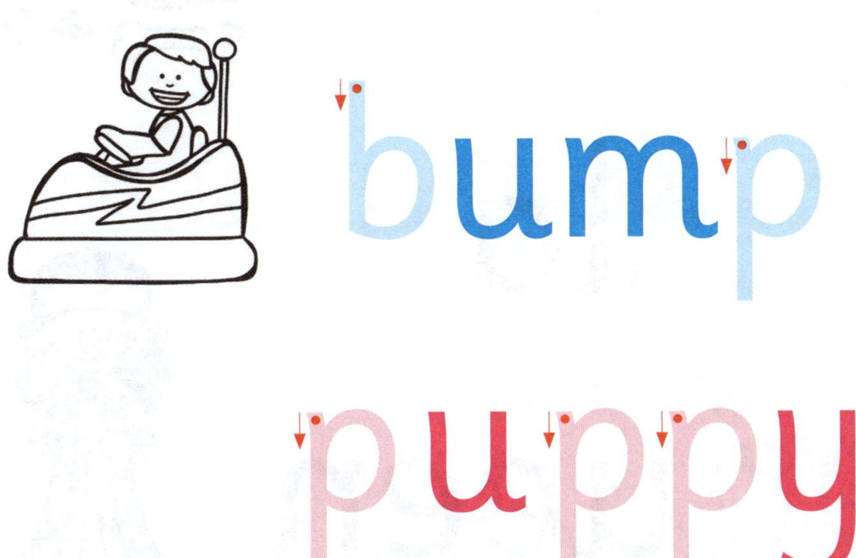

bump

puppy

Great job! Colour the smiley face. 

d, g and q

1 Practise writing these letters that all start with a loop.

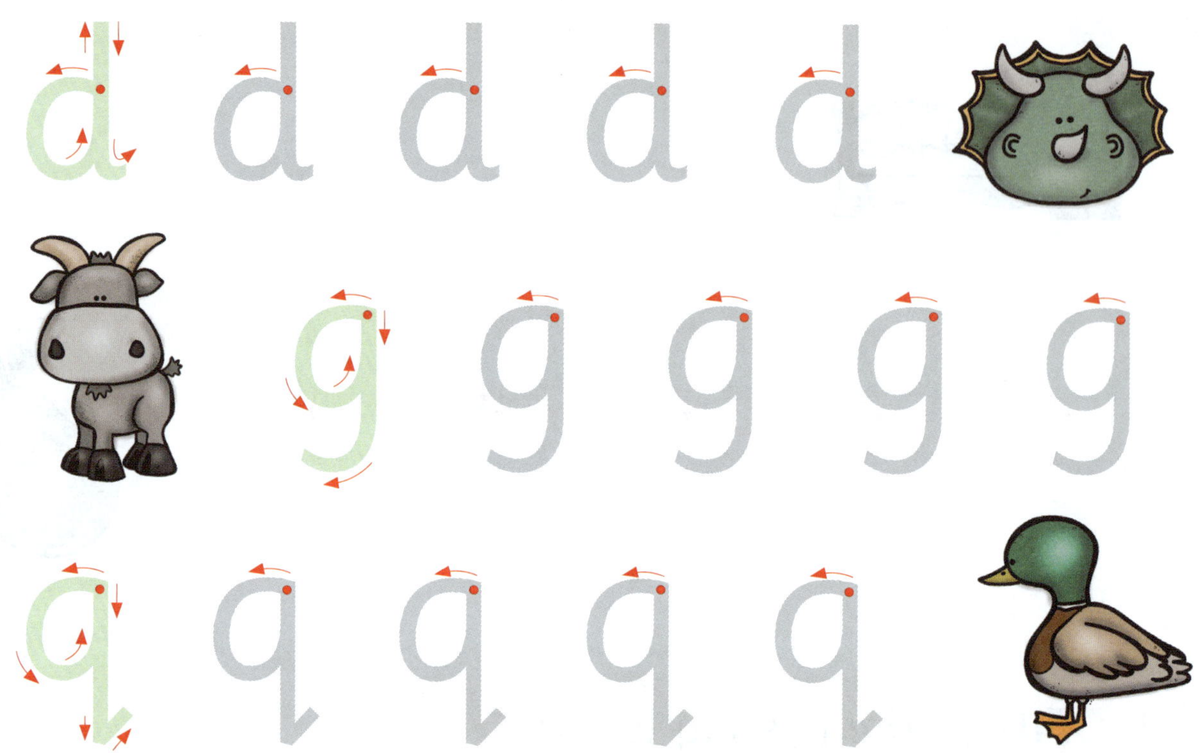

2 **Start** at the red dots and **trace** the letters.

Great job! Colour the smiley face. 

e, s and f

1 **Trace** these three letters that are all curly.

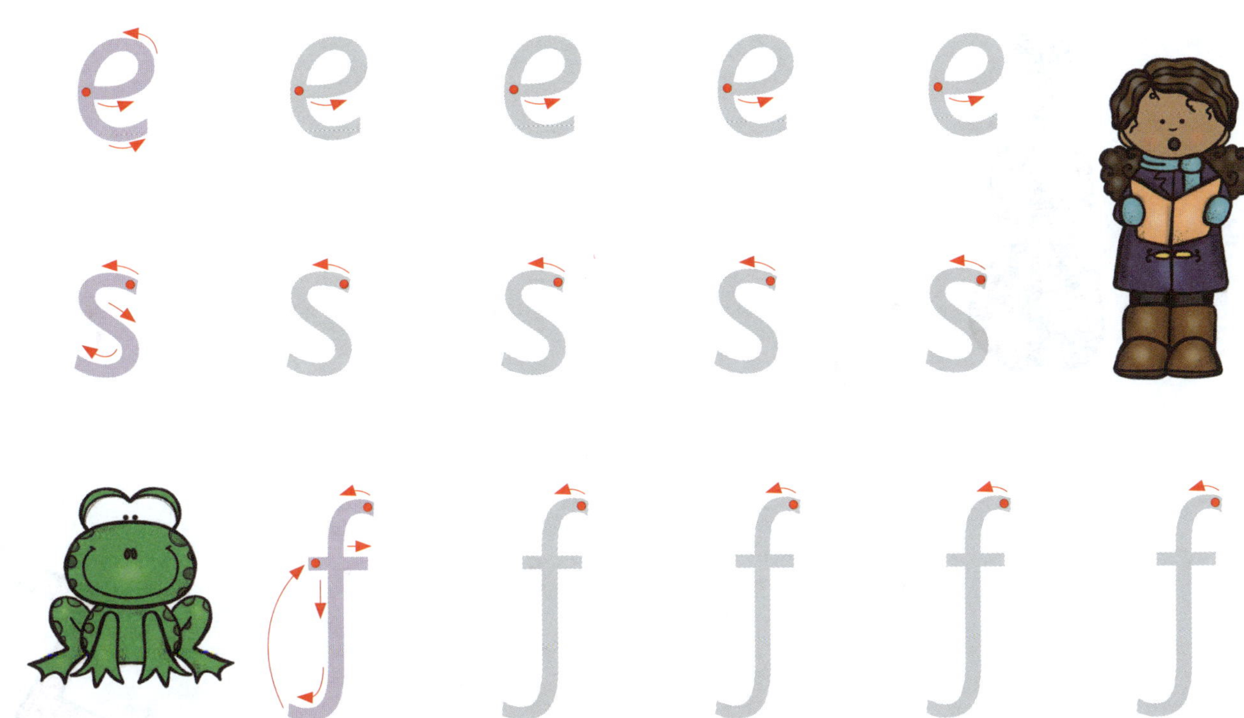

2 **Fill in** the missing letters.

Great job! Colour the smiley face.

v, w, x and z

1 Practise writing the letters **v**, **w**, **x** and **z**.

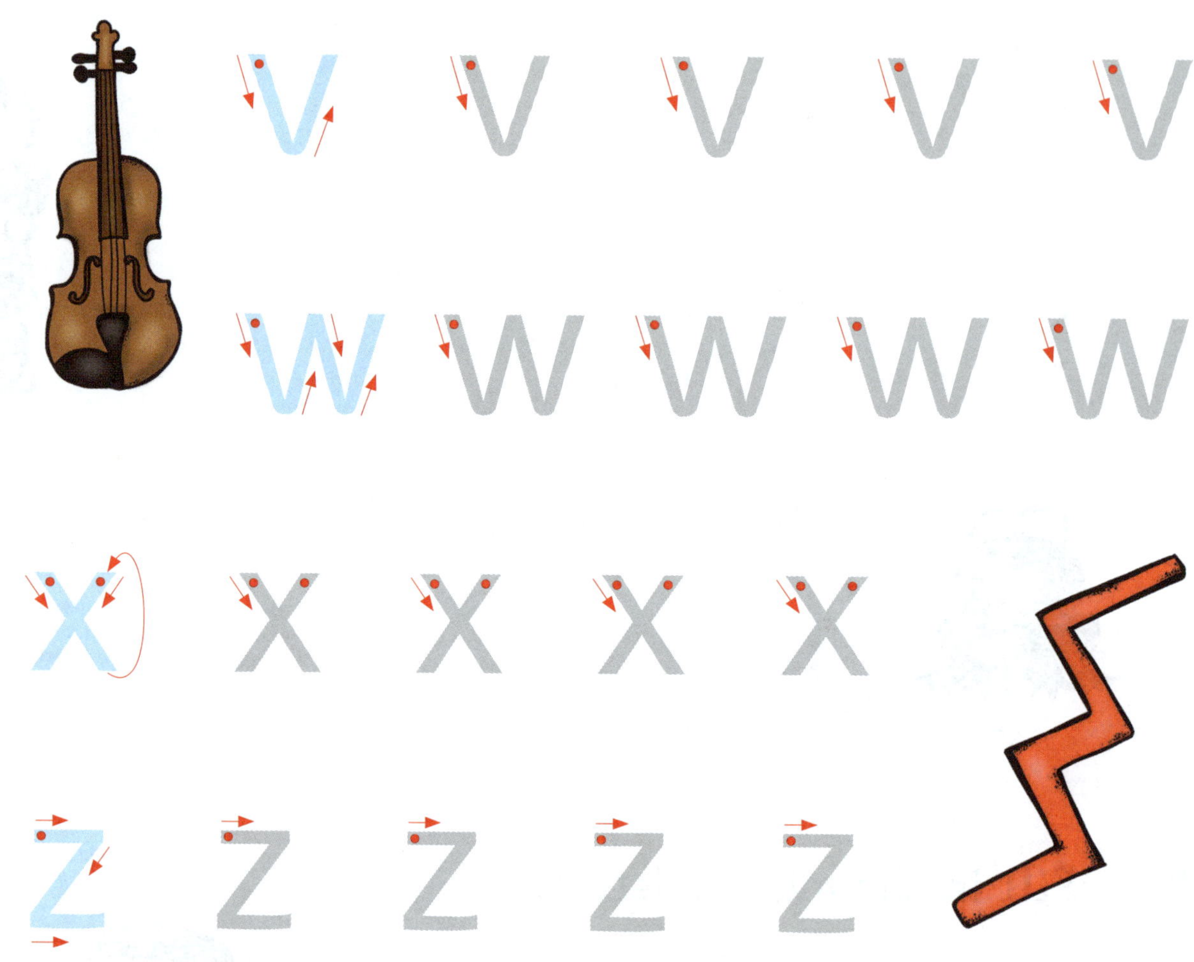

2 **Trace** the missing letters as neatly as you can.

Great job! Colour the smiley face.

Capital Letters

1 Practise writing the capital letters.

Great job! Colour the smiley face.

Numbers

(1) **Practise** writing the numbers below.

0 0 0 0

1 1 1 1

2 2 2 2

3 3 3 3

4 4 4 4

(2) **Trace** the number, then **colour** that number of shells.

4 shells

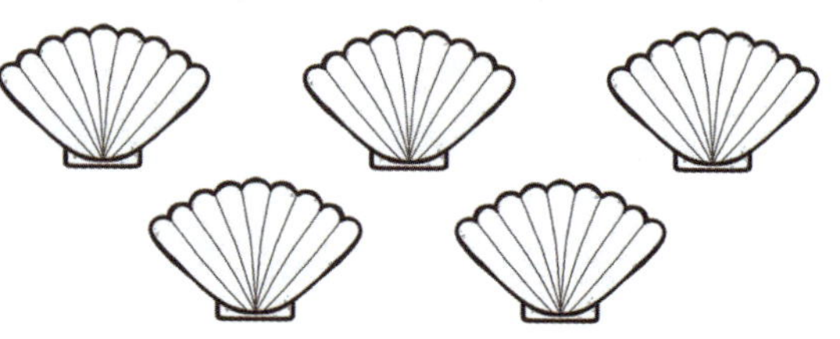

Numbers

3 Trace the numbers to write **5**, **6**, **7**, **8** and **9**.

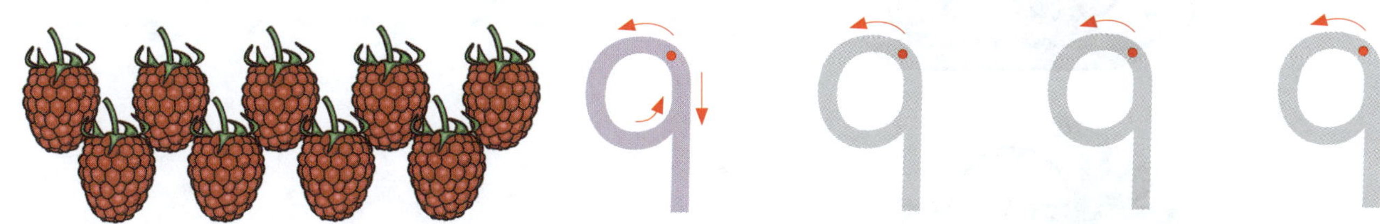

Great job! Colour the smiley face.

Writing Words

(1) **Trace** these words. Remember to **start** each letter with your pencil on the **red dot**.

camp

tent

woods

(2) Now try **tracing** these words.

milk

chicken

turnip

Writing Words

3
Trace these words. Start each letter at the **red dot**.

monster

soft

fuzzy

4
Trace these words, then **colour** the monster.

big

strong

teeth

Writing Words

5 **Trace** these words. Remember to **start** each letter with your pencil on the **red dot**.

fox

sleep

little

6 **Trace** these words. **Draw** lines to match each word to the right picture.

path

owl

nest

Writing Words

7 **Trace** these words. **Start** each letter at the **red dot**.

runner

fast

start

8 **Trace** these words, then **colour in** the medal.

jump

clap

winner

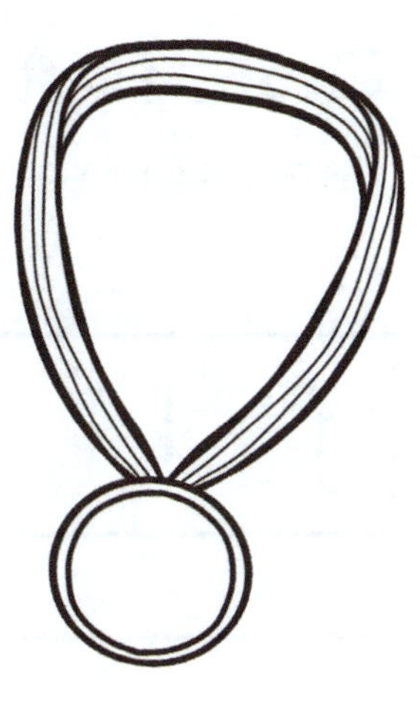

Great job! Colour the smiley face. 

Progress Test 2

1 **Trace** these words.

herbs
seeds

2 marks

2 **Colour** the letters that are missing from the phrase.

silver f__l

oi

ow

1 mark

3 **Choose** letters to complete each word. Then **write** the letters in the **word frame**.

| f | l | | t |
| t | | th |

ai   igh

ee   igh

2 marks

Progress Test 2

(4) **Circle** the caption that matches the picture.

a pair of lunchboxes

a floating ship

1 mark

(5) **Tick** the word that is missing from the sentence.

It has ____ hump.

one ☐

out ☐

1 mark

(6) **Trace** these words. **Draw** lines to match each word to the right picture.

torch

frogs

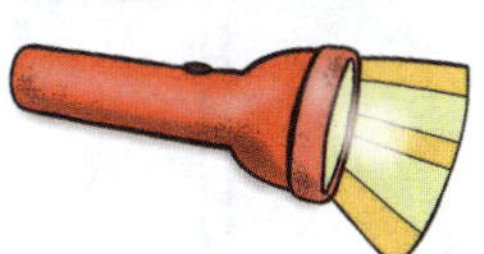

3 marks

Progress Test 2

(7) **Trace** the words below.

the butter
is soft

2 marks

(8) **Blend** the sounds to make the **word**. Then **write** the word in the **word frame**.

| s | p | r | i | n | t |

| | | | | | |

1 mark

(9) **Write** the sentence in the **word frames**.

He has a beard.

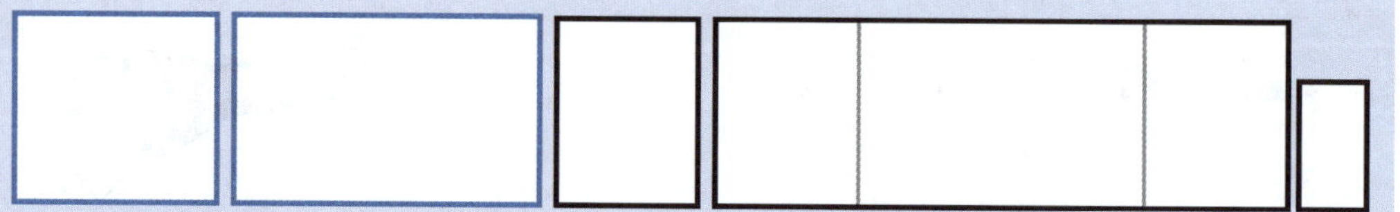

1 mark

Progress Test 2

(10) **Read** the speech bubble. What do you think will happen **next**? **Tick** the right picture.

1 mark

(11) **Read** what Ben says. Which book do you think Ben will choose? **Circle** your answer.

1 mark

Score: ___/16

Answers

Pages 2-3 — Before You Start

1) You should have coloured the dog, the snake and the turtle. (1 mark for each correct answer)
2) You should have circled the book. (1 mark)
3) You should have ticked the mouse. (1 mark)
4) You should have circled the peas. (1 mark)
5) You should have circled the football. (1 mark)
6) The lines should be drawn neatly between the red dots. (1 mark for each correctly drawn line)

Page 4 — s, a and t

1) You should have circled the sandwich.
2) You should have coloured the table.
3) You should have ticked the ant and the anchor.

Page 5 — p, i and n

1) You should have ticked the penguin.
2) You should have circled **n**.
3) igloo — i
    parrot — p

Page 6 — m, d and g

Warm Up:

1) You should have ticked the doughnut.
2) You should have circled the magnet, the guitar, the dolphin and the mountain.

Page 7 — o, c and k

1)

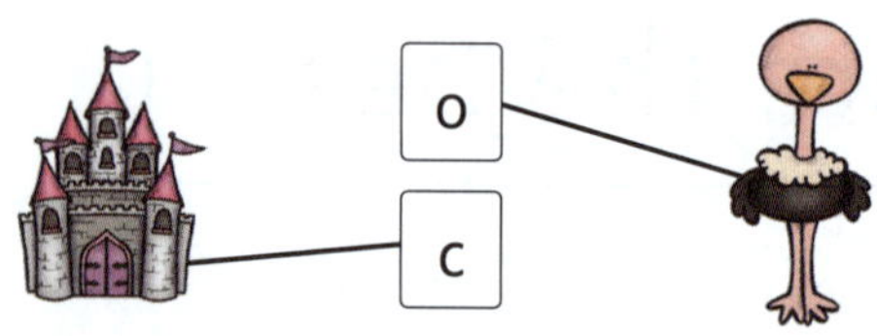

2) You should have coloured the king.
3) octopus — o
    key — k
    kennel — k
    cake — c

Page 8 — ck, e and u

1) You should have circled the clock, the tick and the duck.
2) p**e**g
    c**u**p

Page 9 — r, h and b

Warm Up:

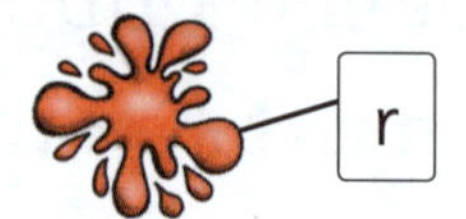 

1) You should have ticked the heart and the helicopter.
2) bear — b
    rainbow — r

Page 10 — f, l, ff, ll and ss

1) lemon — l
    football — f
2) You should have coloured the bell.
3)

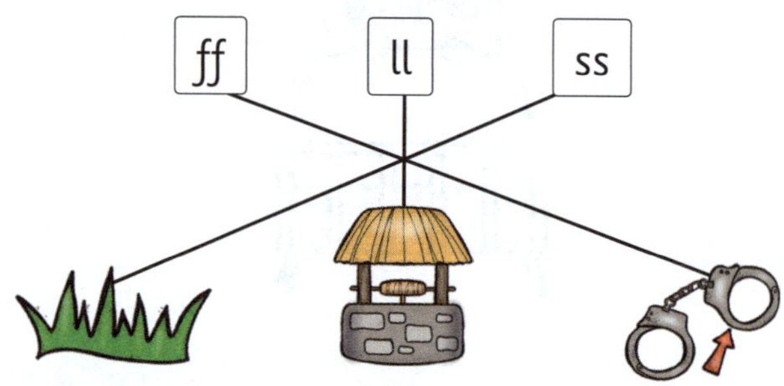

Page 11 — j, v and w

Warm Up: You should have ticked the vase.
1) You should have circled the volcano, the window, the witch and the jelly.
2) van — v
    jam — j

Page 12 — x, y, z, and zz

1) You should have circled the box.
2)

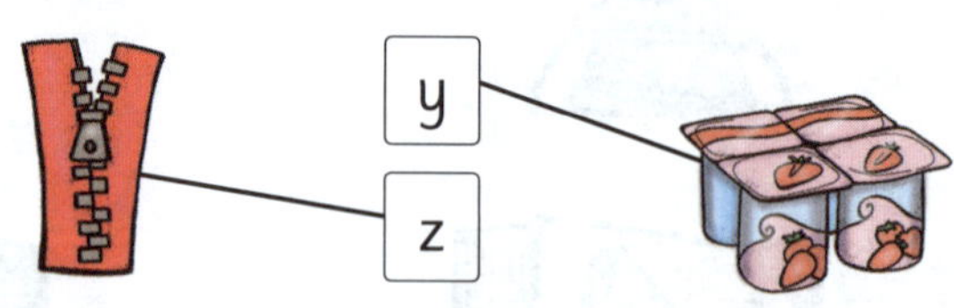

3) bu**zz**
    f**i**x

Page 13 — qu, ch and sh

Warm Up: You should have circled the queen.

Answers

1)

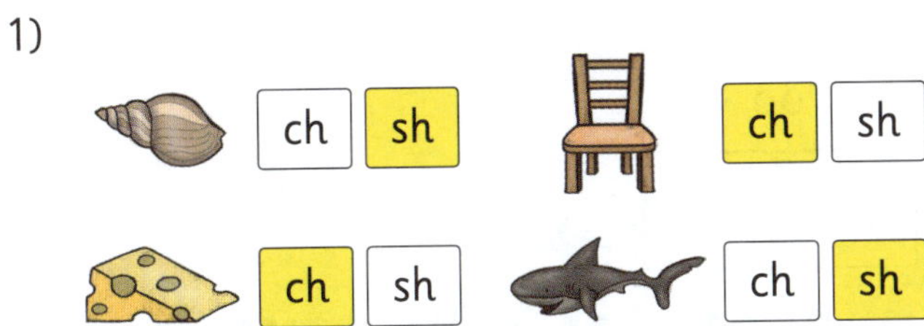

ch **sh**   **ch** sh

ch sh   ch **sh**

2) You should have coloured **quick**.

Page 14 — th, ng and nk

1) You should have coloured the bath.
2) You should have ticked the swing.
3) You should have circled the wink and the sink.

Pages 15-17 — Word Practice

1)

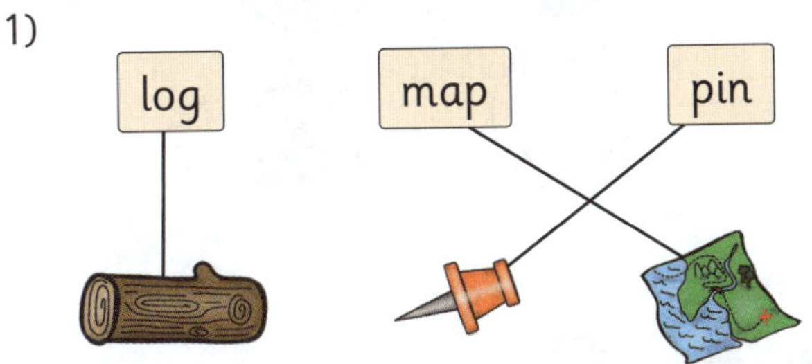

log   map   pin

2) cot
back
doll

3)

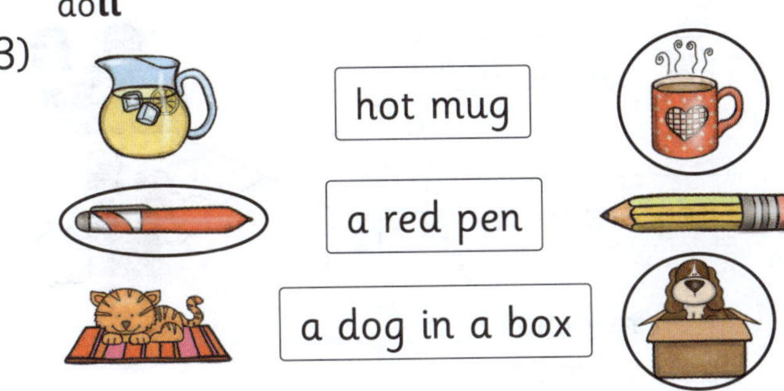

hot mug

a red pen

a dog in a box

4) You should have ticked:
Ella kicks it and **dig in the mud**

5)

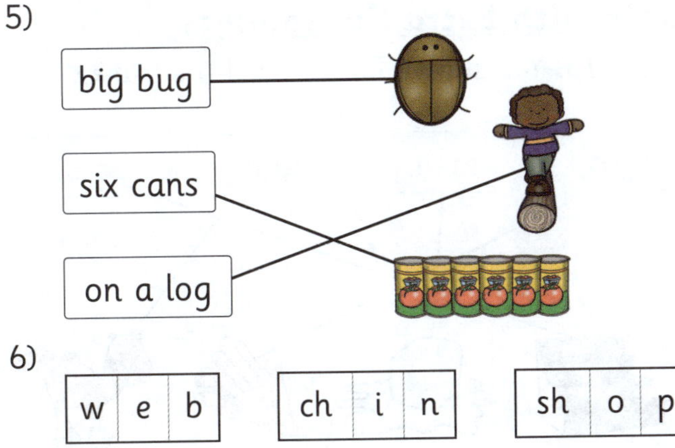

big bug

six cans

on a log

6)

w	e	b

ch	i	n

sh	o	p

Pages 18-19 — Tricky Words

1)

his cat

top of the hill

2)

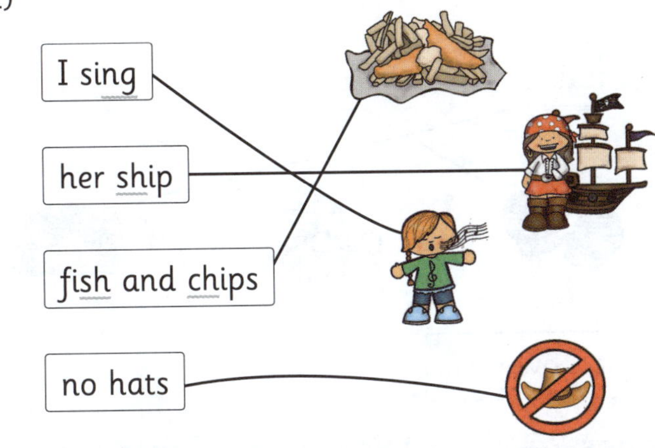

I sing

her ship

fish and chips

no hats

3)

She is sad.

Go into the hut.

4) go **to** bed
we can chat
rich **as** a queen

Page 20 — ai, ee and igh

Warm Up: You should have circled the tail.

1) night — **igh**
chain — **ai**
2) s**ee**d

Page 21 — oa, oo and ar

1) You should have coloured the goat,
the moon and the foot.

2)

c	ar	d
m	ar	ch

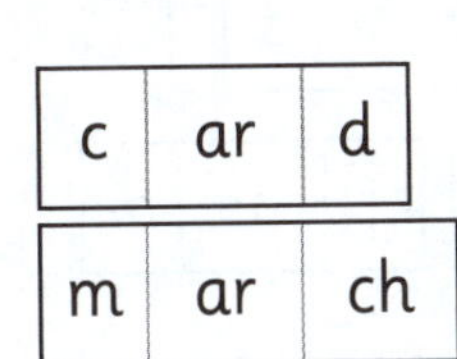

Answers

Page 22 — or, ur, ow and oi

1)

2) You should have circled **burn** and **owl**.

3) s**oi**l
c**oi**ns

Page 23 — ear, air and er

1) You should have circled the tear.

2)

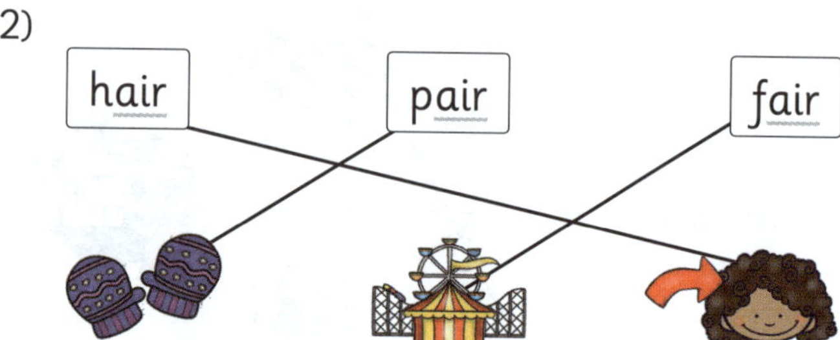

hair	pair	fair

3)

t	ow	er

Pages 24-25 — Words and Sentences

Warm Up:
You should have coloured **visit the zoo**.

1)

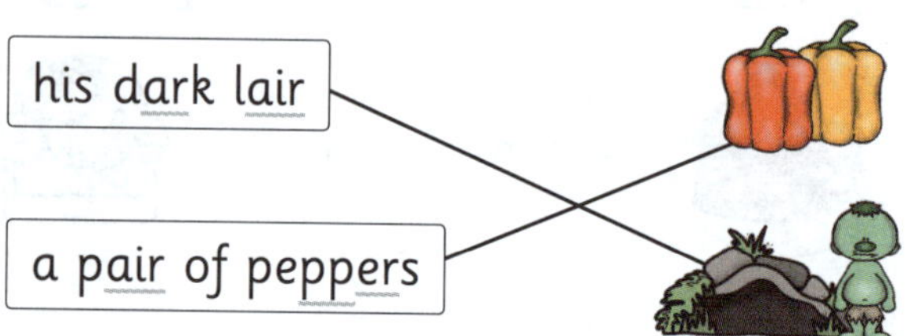

his dark lair

a pair of peppers

2)

I am in the rain.

Meg misses her coat.

The lord is in the fort.

3)

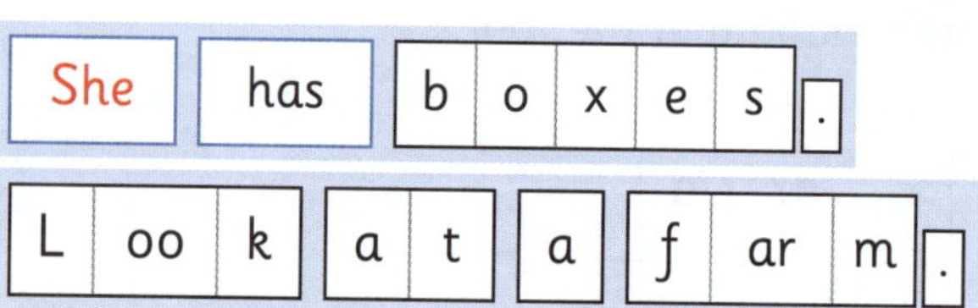

She	has	b	o	x	e	s	.

L	oo	k	a	t	a	f	ar	m	.

4)

c	oo	k
s	ur	f

Pages 26-27 — More Tricky Words

1)

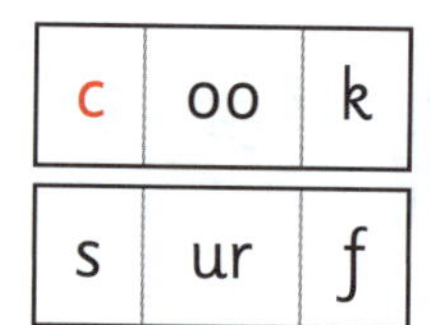

me

sure

pure

2) You should have ticked:

3)

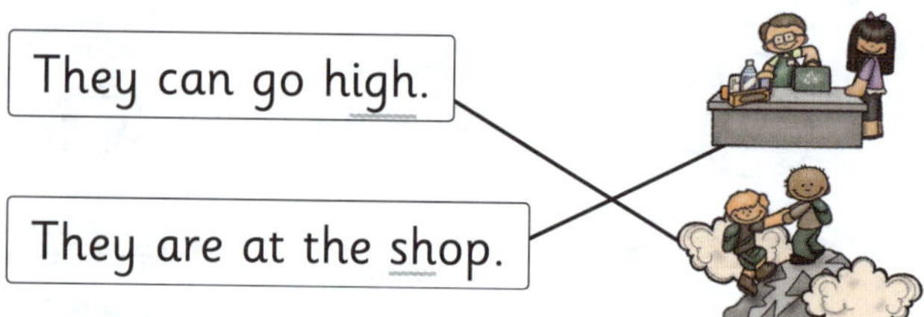

They can go high.

They are at the shop.

4) I sit on **my** chair.
Can **you** see it?
The car **was** pink.

Pages 28-29 —
Words with Extra Consonants

Warm Up: You should have circled the trunk.

1)

clap	melt	hump	stair

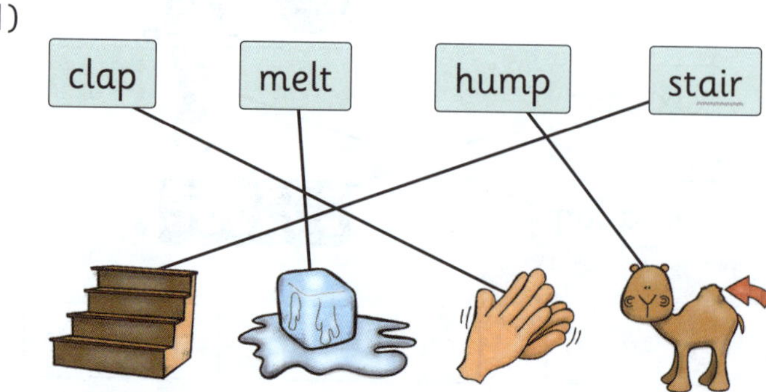

2) You should have coloured **street** and **crust**.

Answers

3) You should have ticked **sport** and **start**.
4) You should have circled **toothbrush**.
5)

g	r	ow	l	
s	p	r	i	ng

Pages 30-31 — More Words and Sentences

1)

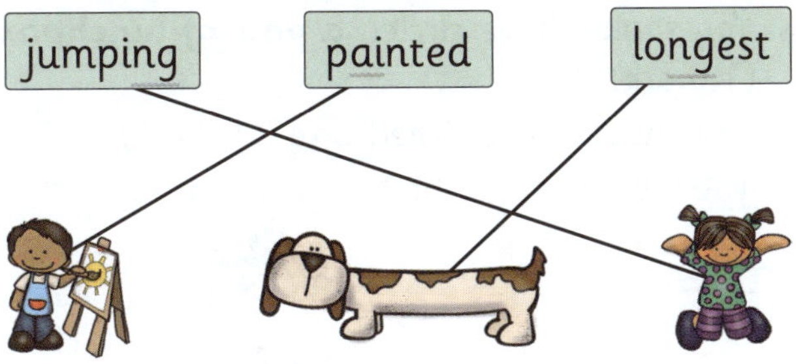

2)

g	r	a	n	
s	p	o	t	
t	w	i	n	s

3)

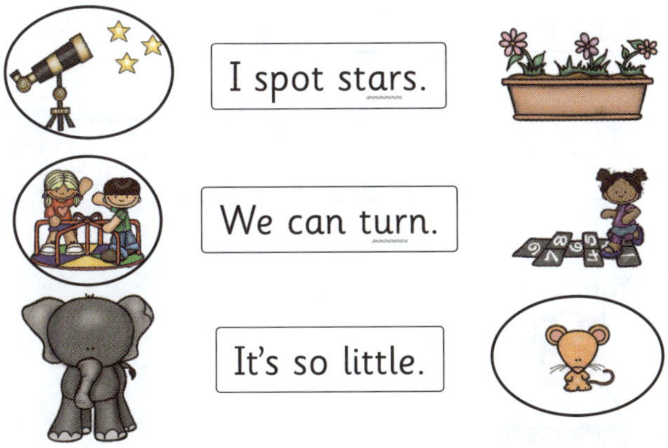

4)

s	i	nk	i	ng	
s	l	ee	p	i	ng

Pages 32-33 — More Tricky Words

Warm Up:
You should have coloured **some sweets**.

1)

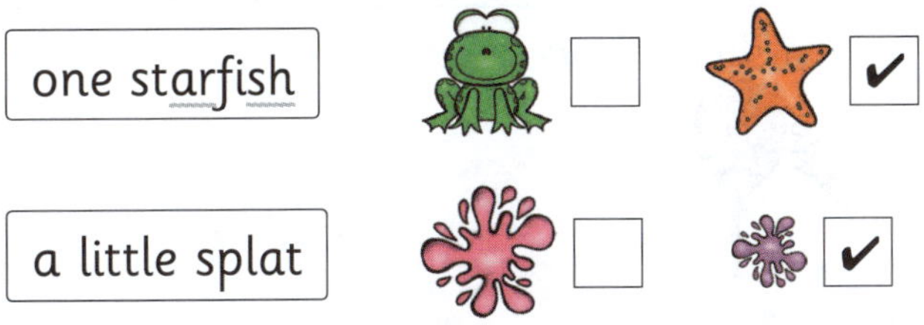

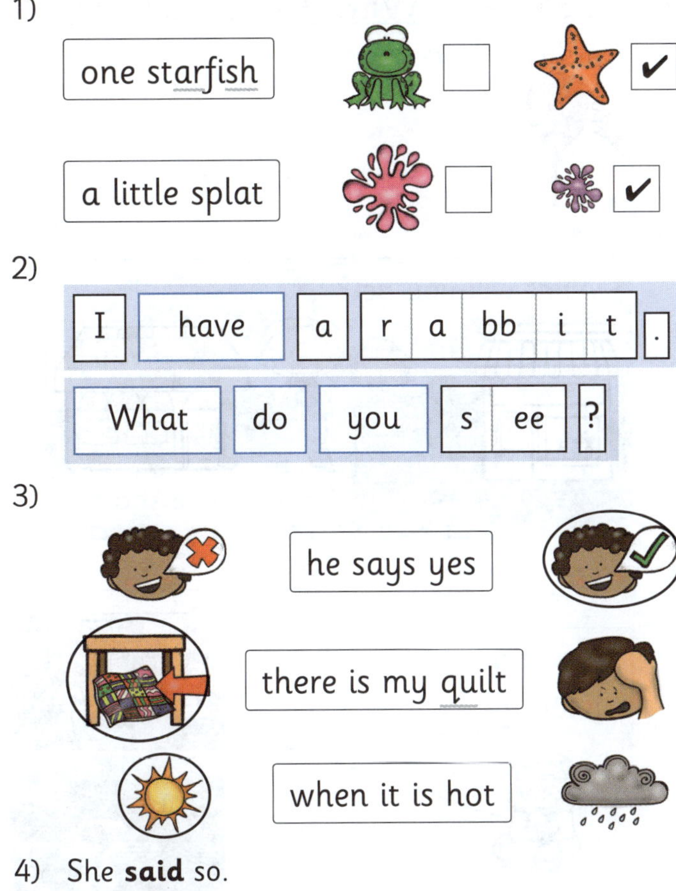

2)

I	have	a	r	a	bb	i	t	.
What	do	you	s	ee	?			

3)

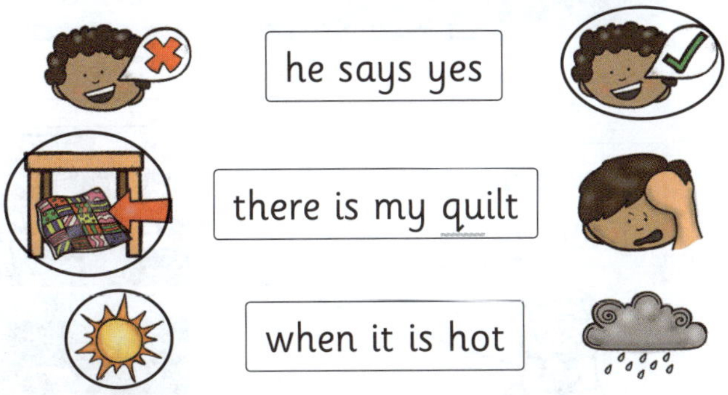

4) She **said** so.
They **were** sad.
I **love** my dress.

Pages 34-37 — Understanding Stories

Warm Up: You should have circled:

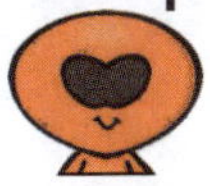

1) You should have circled:

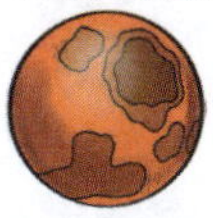

2) You should have circled:

3) You should have coloured **They had a fright.**
4) You should have circled **no**.
5) You should have ticked:

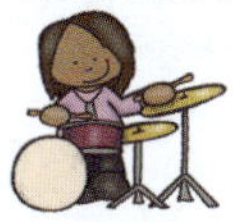

6) You should have coloured the guitar.
7) You should have circled **yes**.
8) You should have circled the torch.

Answers

Pages 38-39 — What Happens Next?

1) You should have ticked:

2)

3)

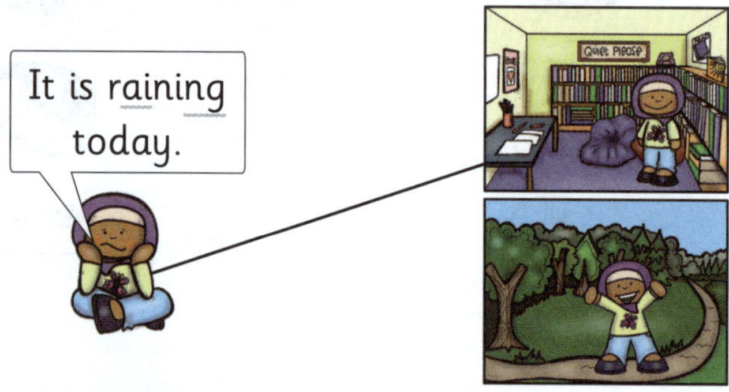

4) You should have circled:

Pages 40-41 — Progress Test 1

1) You should have ticked **summer**. (1 mark)

2)

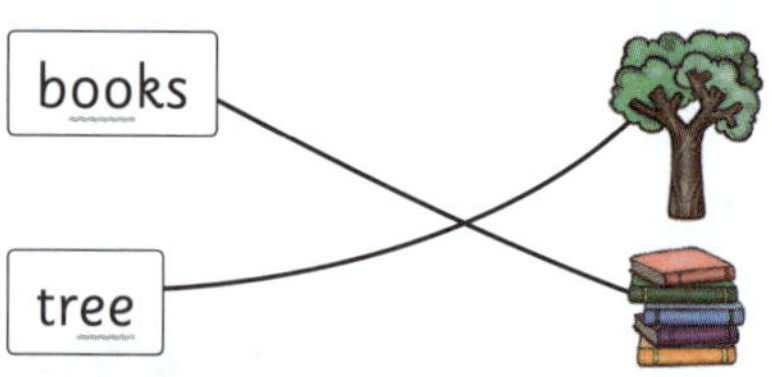

(1 mark)

3) You should have circled:

(1 mark)

4) You should have coloured the tree and the bee.
(1 mark for each correct answer)

5) You should have ticked **He is running.**
(1 mark)

6) You should have coloured **to**. (1 mark)

Pages 60-63 — Progress Test 2

1) The words should be correctly traced.
(1 mark for each word written correctly)

2) You should have coloured **oi**. (1 mark)

3) fl**igh**t
t**ee**th
(1 mark for each correct answer)

4) You should have circled **a pair of lunchboxes**.
(1 mark)

5) You should have ticked **one**. (1 mark)

6) The words should be correctly traced.

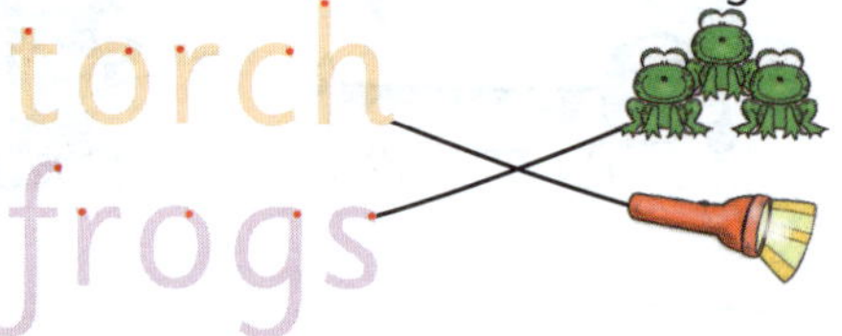

(1 mark for each word written correctly, 1 mark
for correctly matching the pictures and words)

7) The words should be correctly traced.
(1 mark if most letters are traced correctly,
2 marks if all letters are traced correctly)

8)

s	p	r	i	n	t

(1 mark)

9)

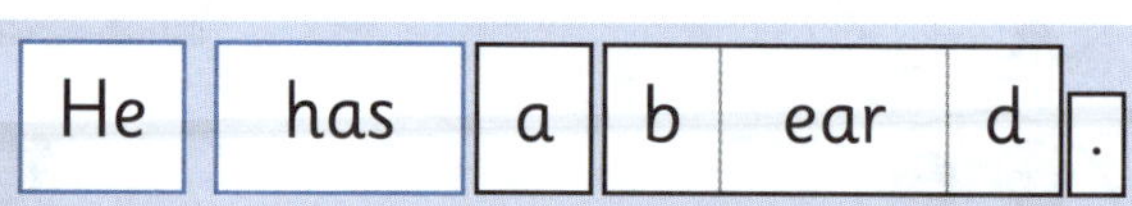

(1 mark)

10) You should have ticked:

(1 mark)

11) You should have circled:

(1 mark)